The three little pigs

Look at the pictures and read the story of the three little pigs.

Once upon a time there were three little pigs who lived at home.

One day Mummy Pig said to them, “You are getting big now so you must go and build your own house. Make sure that the big, bad wolf cannot get you.”

So the three little pigs set off and saw a man carrying straw. The first little pig decided he wanted to build his house from straw.

He wondered where to begin and needed some help.

Activity 1

Straw

Can you help the first little pig make a house out of straw?

You will need

pieces of straw

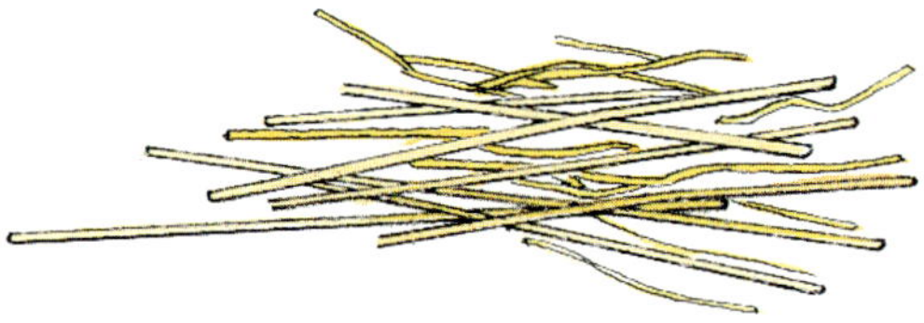

Look at pieces of straw. Feel the straw.

Ask yourself questions.

* Would straw be strong enough for a house?
* Would you like to live in a house of straw?
* Have you seen any houses made of straw?
* How strong is the straw?
* Why would anyone build a house of straw?

Test the strength of straw.
Take a bundle of two or three strands:

pull it

twist it

squash it

cut it

Take a thicker bundle. Do the same tests.

Activity 2

Making a straw house

Take some bundles of straw and make a model of a house out of it.

Make the straw stronger.

- Can you find ways of making the straw stand up?
- Can you find ways of making the straw stick together?
- Can you finds ways of preventing the straw from breaking?

Have you tried:

using string with the straw

using plasticine with the straw

Test the different ways you have found of making the straw stronger.
Remember who the house is for and what it is for.

Ask yourself:

- How big is the pig?
- How will he get into the house?
- How will the house keep the wolf out?
- Which shape of house stands up best?

Activity 3

Testing the straw houses

You will need
a hairdryer

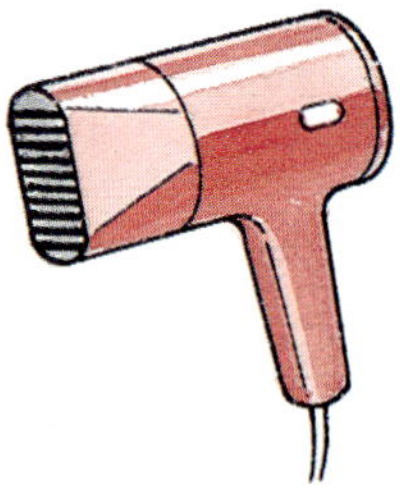

Look at all the houses your class have made.

Tell the other children the problems you had.
How did you solve them?

Read the story.

Now when the first little pig was in bed in his straw house that night, he heard some terrible words, "Little pig, little pig, let me come in."

It was the big, bad wolf. So the little pig shouted, "No, no, I will not let you in."

The wolf said,

"I can huff, I can puff, I can blow your house down."

Pretend to be the wolf.
Say the words and use a hairdryer on the straw houses.

- What do you find?
- Is straw a good material for building?

All kinds of wood

The second little pig met a man carrying some sticks. This gave him an idea. He would build his house with sticks of wood.

First he would find out about wood.
Help the second little pig collect different kinds of wood.
Look outside and inside.

Collect
things made from wood

Where else do you think you could find wood for building the second little pig's home?

Handle all the different kinds of wood. How do they feel? Think about how they look. You can smooth off rough corners of wood with sandpaper to make it smooth.

Do you feel how hot the wood becomes when it is rubbed very hard?

Make a display of the wood you have collected.

Activity 5

Design and build a house with sticks

You will need

collection of wooden objects

We have to build a house out of sticks.
Look at the wooden objects you have collected in your classroom.

Ask yourself questions.

* What kind of wood would be best to build with? Test the wood by sawing, scratching and bending.

Be careful

* How can you make your house stand up? What shapes are best to do this? Tall shapes? Short shapes?
* What ways are there of joining objects together?

You will need

Communicating

You will need
painting materials

Draw or paint your wooden house on a piece of paper. Write a short sentence about your house.

Talk about your houses with the rest of the class.

- What problems did you have in making it?
- How did you try and solve them?

Activity 7

Testing the house made with sticks

The house needs to stand up to forces.

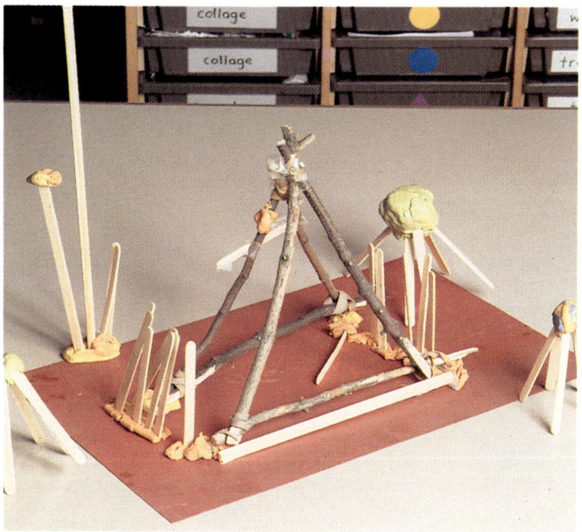

What different forces can you think of, which the house needs to withstand?

- the huffing and puffing of the wolf
- heavy snow falling on the roof
- the blowing of the wind (see page 13)

Read the story.

> The wolf came to the second little pig's house when he was asleep. He said, "Little pig, little pig, let me come in."
>
> The little pig shouted, "No!"
>
> So the wolf said, "I can huff, I can puff, I can blow the house down."

You will need
a hairdryer

Pretend to be the wolf. Use the hairdryer on the wooden house. What happens?

Experiment with the position of the hairdryer.
Does it matter if you blow on one house from far away and on another from nearby?
Are the forces different if the hairdryer is switched on fast or slow?

The third little pig

The third little pig still needs to build a house. What can he use?

Think up some ideas to solve his problem.

Look at the school building.
Make a list of all the materials it is made of.
Would your school keep out the wolf?

Collect building materials.

Plastic:	hard, soft, shapes, sheets, tubes
Metal:	tubes, sheet, wire, rods
Bricks:	different types, lego, wooden
Concrete:	slabs
Wood:	planks, sticks

Make a class display of building materials.

Activity 9

All about bricks

Play with some wooden bricks of different sizes and shapes.

Can you build the third little pig's house with these bricks?

Plan your house. Ask yourself questions.

* How tall will the house have to be?

Make tall houses and low houses. Which would be stronger? Give each one a push to see or test with a hairdryer.

* How wide will the house have to be?

Make narrow houses and wide houses. How many pigs will fit into each?

Which way of building with the bricks will make the house stronger?
Look outside at how brick walls are put together.
Look at the patterns or bonding of the bricks.
Try out some of the ideas that you see with lego bricks.

Testing the brick house

Read the story:

Now the third little pig pretended to be asleep that night in his new brick house. He was frightened but brave.

The wolf came up to his house and howled, "Little pig, little pig, let me come in."

The pig shouted, "No, no. I will not let you in!"

The wolf said,

"I can huff, I can puff, I can blow the house down."

You will need
a hairdryer

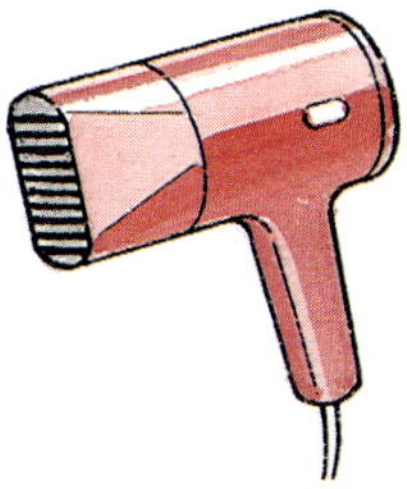

Test how strong the house is by using the hairdryer on it.

Decide where you want to position the hairdryer.

What happens?

And the third little pig was A CLEVER LITTLE PIG!

Activity 11

A closer look at bricks

You will need

Put a brick into water.

* Where do the bubbles come from?
* Does it happen with wooden bricks?
* Can you choose bricks which will give a lot of bubbles or fewer bubbles?

Place a brick in a small amount of water.
Watch the water rise up the brick.

Stand another brick on top and see if the water will rise up through that one too.

Now we have another problem.
Can you think what it is?

Forces: the wind

Think about the wind.

Go outside.

Try running with the wind.
against the wind.

Look for clues of the wind at work.

Look for:

- people's long hair blowing around
- objects blowing across the street
- wind damage on buildings such as slates or tiles blown off roofs
- leaves on trees fluttering

How do all these things move?

Go inside.
Blow on some objects.
Try staws, sticks, a lego brick.

- What happens to each one?
- Where do they move to?

Activity 13

Visiting a building site

You have built three houses, so you are a builder.
Find out more about builders who make life-size houses and buildings.

Visit a building site.

Be careful ⚠

What people do you see on a building site?

A bricklayer

A painter

A plasterer

A carpenter

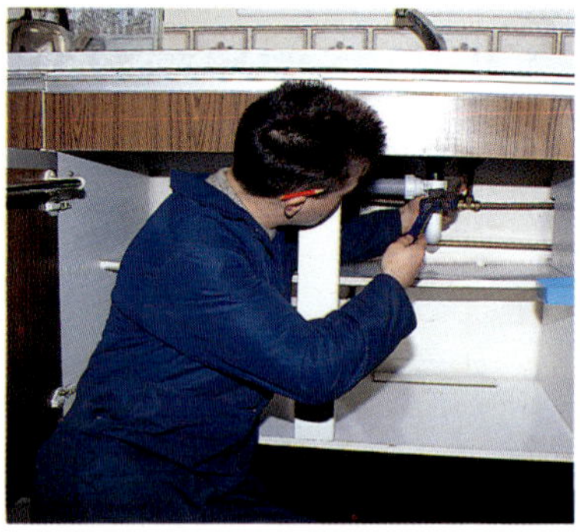

A plumber

- What are their jobs?
- What tools do they each use?
- What special clothes do they wear? Why?

Make a class display of tools and building clothes.

Machines on building sites

How many different machines can you see on the building site? Be a good detective!

* What are they used for?
* Where are they placed?

Look for:

A concrete mixer

A crane

A drill

A simple pulley

* What makes each one move? Talk about it as a class.

Design a machine which will lift something.

You will need construction kits

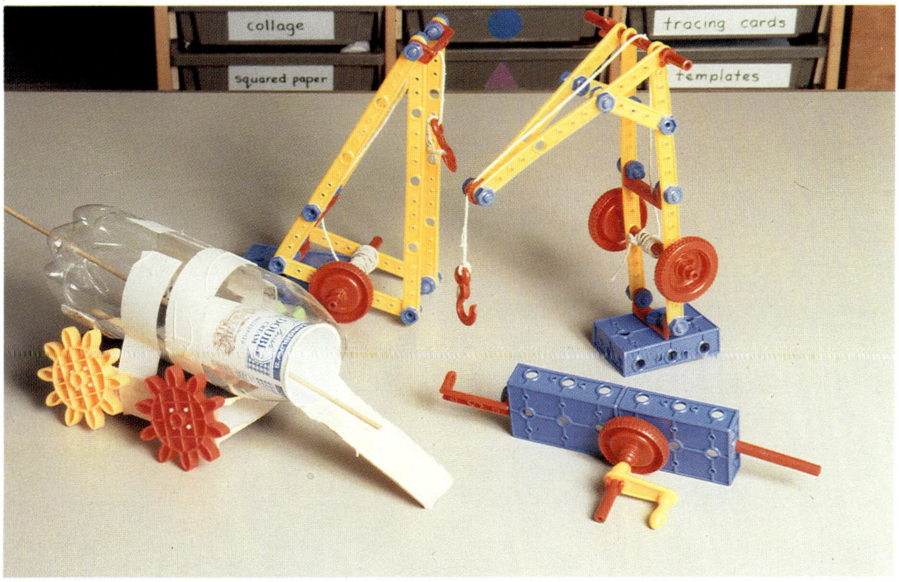

Activity 15

Building site problems

Problem

We need to move a heavy object up onto a higher level.

You will need

a toy wheelbarrow

a few bricks

Fill a toy wheelbarrow with bricks and place it near a step.
How are you going to get the wheelbarrow up on to the step?

Think of some solutions to the problem.
Test some of the ideas out.

A ramp is a good idea.

You will need

a plank of wood

Find the right angle at which to place the plank.

- ✱ Did you see any ramps at the building site?
- ✱ Have you seen any in other places?
- ✱ How do they help people?